HABBER-JABBER-LAW

A Nonsense Adventure

Translated by

ARUNAVA SINHA

Sukumar Ray was a poet, short-story writer and playwright who wrote in Bengali mainly for children. His works such as the collection of nonsense poems *Abol Tabol,* novella *Hojoborolo,* short-story collection *Pagla Dashu* and play *Chalachittachanchari* are considered some of the finest writing for children in the world.

Arunava Sinha translates classic, modern and contemporary Bengali fiction, non-fiction and poetry into English. Forty of his translations have been published so far. Born and educated in Calcutta, he lives and writes in Delhi.

Sudeshna Shome Ghosh is an editor. She is also co-founder of Cosy Nook Library, a children's library in Bangalore. She has written and translated books for children.

THE WONDERFUL NONSENSE WORLD OF SUKUMAR RAY

Habber-Jabber-Law and Other Stories and Poems

Translated by

ARUNAVA SINHA

SUDESHNA SHOME GHOSH

talking CUB

An Imprint of Speaking Tiger Books

TALKING CUB

Published by Speaking Tiger Books LLP
125A, Ground Floor, Shahpur Jat,
Near Asiad Village, New Delhi - 110 049

Habber-Jabber-Law first published by Talking Cub, an imprint of Speaking Tiger Books, in 2020

Dashu's Mystery Box, Crackers in a Pot, No Fear, Come Here and *Don't Laugh, Ramgoru Calf* first published by Storyweaver, a digital platform for children's books by Pratham Books

This collection published by Talking Cub, an imprint of Speaking Tiger Books, in 2024

ISBN: 978-93-5447-767-6

eISBN: 978-93-5447-952-6

10 9 8 7 6 5 4 3 2 1

The moral right of the author has been asserted.
Typeset in Crimson Text by Jojy Philip
Printed at Chaman Enterprises, New Delhi

Contents

It was ridiculously hot. There I was, lying down quietly in the shade beneath the tree, but the sweat was killing me. My handkerchief was somewhere on the grass. Just as I was about to pick it up to wipe my face, it said, 'Miaow!' So annoying. Why was the handkerchief going miaow?

When I looked at it, the handkerchief wasn't a handkerchief anymore; there was a plump, tawny cat with flaring whiskers in its place, trying to stare me down. I said, 'Houston, we have a problem. Was a 'kerchief, now it's a cat chief.' At once the cat responded, 'I don't see a problem. Was an egg, now it's a healthy, quack-quack duck. Happens all the time.'

After some thought, I said, 'What do I call you then? You're not really a cat, after all. You're a handkerchief.' The cat said, 'You can call me cat chief, you can call me kerchief, you can even call me capital zed.'

'Capital zed?' I asked. 'Why capital zed?'

At this the cat snorted, 'You're telling me you don't even know that?' Then it shut one eye and began to laugh in a most irritating manner.

I wasn't prepared for this. I felt I should at least have understood the bit about the capital zed. I was so flustered I blurted out, 'Oh yes, got it now.'

The cat was mighty pleased. 'Yes, it's obvious—G for capital zed, L for cat, ASSES for those who use handkerchiefs, and what do you get? GLASSES. 'Amiright?'

I didn't get a word of any this, but because the cat jumped into a tree and began laughing again in the most disgusting fashion, I just went along with 'mm-hmm, mm-hmm'.

Now the cat gazed at the sky for some time before saying, 'If you're hot why don't you just go to Tibet?'

'That's easy to say, but it's not like I can just up and go,' I told him.

'Why not? What's the problem?'

'Do you know how to get there?' I asked in return.

A smile spread across the cat's face. 'Of course, I do. Calcutta, Dibrugarh, Rimbik, Tibet. That's all there is to it. Direct journey. Takes an hour and a quarter. You can go any time you like.'

'Can you give me directions then?'

At this the cat looked strangely grave. 'Uh-huh, not up to me. If Bigtree

Bro were here, he'd have given you the right directions.'

'Who's Bigtree Bro? Where does he live?'

The cat said, 'Where do you suppose Bigtree Bro lives? In the trees, of course.'

'Where can I meet him then?'

The cat began to shake his head vehemently. 'No chance, you're not getting to meet him.'

'How do you mean?'

'You want to know what it's like? Imagine you turn up in Ulhasnagar to meet him, but he's in Mangaluru at that time. If you rush to Mangaluru, you'll find he's in Raipur. And when you go there, you discover he's gone off to

Kohima. There's absolutely no chance of meeting him.'

'Then how do any of you get to meet him?'

'It's most complicated. First you have to figure out the places where bro isn't; then you have to work out the places where he might be; then you have to find out where bro is right now. Then you have to calculate using these results where bro will be when you get to a particular place at a particular time. After that you have to find out...'

Interrupting the cat, I asked, 'What sort of calculations are you talking about?'

The cat said, 'Very difficult calculations. Want to see?' Taking a stick, he drew a long line across the grass. 'Let's say this is Bigtree Bro.' Then he sat in silence with a grave expression for a long time. After this he drew an identical line and said, 'Let's say this is you,' and lapsed into silence again, cocking his head on one side. Then another line, followed by, 'Let's say this is capital zed.' And so he went on, alternating long periods of reflection with a long line drawn across the grass and saying, 'Let's say this is Tibet'... 'Let's say this is Bigtree Bro's wife cooking in the kitchen'... 'Let's say this is a hollow in a tree trunk...'

Listening to him drone on, I suddenly found my temper rising. 'Such rubbish!' I shouted. 'What rot is all this, I can't make head or tail of it.' The cat nodded. 'Okay, let me make it simpler. Shut your eyes and do the maths with the numbers I give you.' I closed my eyes obediently.

And there I was, with my eyes closed, still waiting, but not a peep out of the cat. Suddenly I became suspicious, and sure enough, when I opened my eyes, it was to see the cat leaping over the fence and running away with its tail upright, sniggering all the while.

That was that. I sat down on a rock beneath the tree, and at once someone said hoarsely, 'Seven twos are?'

Who was this now? I was looking around in search of the voice when it came again, 'Why don't you answer? Seven twos are?' Looking up into the tree, I found a raven writing something on a schoolchild's slate with a piece of chalk, occasionally twisting his neck to throw a glance at me. I said, 'Seven twos are fourteen.' At once the raven began to sway from side to side, saying, 'Wrong, wrong…fail.'

I was livid. 'Of course it's not wrong. Seven ones are seven, seven twos are fourteen, seven threes are twenty-one.' Instead of answering, the raven began to suck on his pencil and ponder over something. Then he said, 'Seven twos are fourteen, put down four, carry over the pencil.' I frowned, 'Weren't you saying just now seven twos are *not* fourteen? So you've changed your mind?' The raven replied, 'It hadn't got to fourteen yet when you said it, it was thirteen rupees and ninety-three paise. If I hadn't written down fourteen in the nick of time it would have gone up to fourteen rupees and twenty-one paise by now.'

'I've never seen such ignorance in my

life,' I said. 'If seven twos are fourteen it's always fourteen, whether an hour ago or ten days later.'

The raven was astonished. 'Isn't time money where you live?'

'What do you mean time is money?' I asked.

'You'd get it if you lived here for some time. We're facing high inflation here now, can't afford to waste a second. I have been working so hard and even stealing to save some time these past few days, now I've spent half of it arguing with you.' He resumed his calculations and I sat there wondering what to do now.

Suddenly something slid out of a hollow in the tree and slithered down to the ground. I found a very old man about three feet tall, with a green beard flowing all the way down to his feet, holding a hubble bubble without a bowl or anything—and sporting an enormous bald head. Something was written with a chalk on that hairless pate of his.

Looking like he had a hundred things to do, the old man drew on his hubble bubble a couple of times and asked, 'Done with the accounts?'

The raven looked around and said, 'Almost done.'

The old man said, 'How peculiar! It's been nineteen days and you still haven't managed to complete it?'

The raven sucked on his pencil solemnly for three or four minutes and then asked, 'How many days has it been, did you say?'

The old man said, 'Nineteen.'

At once the raven craned his neck and said, 'Go go go twenty!'

The old man said, 'Twenty-one!'

The raven said, 'Twenty-two.'

The old man said, 'Twenty-three.'

The raven said, 'Twenty-three-and-a-half.'

It was just like an auction. Suddenly the raven looked at me. 'How come you aren't bidding?'

'What on earth should I be bidding for?'

The old man hadn't spotted me all this while. Hearing me speak, he whirled like a top nine or ten times and then turned to me, after which he stared at me through his hubble bubble as though it was a telescope. Then he pulled out some coloured glass discs from his pocket and peered at me through them. Finally, he got hold of a measuring tape from somewhere and began to take my measurements, shouting, 'Length twenty-six inches, sleeves twenty-six inches, cuffs twenty-six inches, chest twenty-six inches, neck twenty-six inches.'

I protested vehemently. 'Impossible. How can the chest and the neck both be twenty-six inches? Am I a pig?'

The old man said, 'Check for yourself if you don't believe me.'

Examining the measuring tape, I discovered all the numbers had been rubbed off, with only the number twenty-six being faintly visible. So whatever the old man measured turned out to be twenty-six inches.

Then he asked me, 'Weight?'

'I don't know.'

Poking me with his fingertips, he said, 'Two kilos and a half.'

I said, 'What! Even Potla weighs twenty-one kilos, and he's a whole year-and-a-half younger than me.'

The raven butted in, 'That's because there's a different way of calculating where you come from.'

The old man nodded, 'Note it down then, weight two kilos and a half, age thirty-seven.'

'Oh please!' I said. 'I'm eight years and three months old, what do you mean thirty-seven.'

The old man chewed on this for a bit and then said, 'Going up or down?'

'What on earth is that?'

The old man explained, 'What I'm

saying is, is your age going up or going down?'

'How can anyone's age go down?'

'Are you suggesting it should go up constantly? I've had it then. One day my age will go up to sixty, seventy, even eighty. Do you want me to die of old age or something?'

'Naturally. Eighty means old age.'

'Fat lot you know. Why should I ever be eighty? We reverse the direction as soon as we reach forty. After that it's not forty-one, forty-two—our age starts dropping, thirty-nine, thirty-eight, thirty-seven. When it's gone all the way down to ten, it's allowed to rise again. Take my age, it's gone up and down so many times, I'm thirteen now.'

I was hysterical with laughter on hearing this.

The raven said, 'Can you speak softly, I need to finish the accounts quickly.'

At once the old man sidled over to sit down next to me, swinging his legs, and whispered, 'I'm going to tell you a marvellous story. Wait, let me make it up.' Scratching his bald head with his hubble bubble, he closed his eyes to think. Then he announced, 'Yes, I've got it. Now listen...

'Now what's happened is that the senior minister had swallowed the princess's needle and thread, but no one had a clue about it. Meanwhile the monster, you know what he did, he rolled over in his bed, still asleep, muttering, "Pell mell dell, is that a man I smell" and fell right off it. And instantly there was banging and clanging and guards and soldiers and men and beasts and ho ho ho hey hey hey grab and kill grab and kill shoot at sight shoot at sight—when suddenly the king spoke up, "If it's a dragon we're talking about, where's the tail?" At this the ministers sinisters officers coffee-sirs surgeons guardians all of them exclaimed, "Good point! Where's the tail?" Naturally, no one could answer, so they all began to sneak out one by one.'

The raven interrupted the story to ask me, 'Got the advertisement? The handbill?'

I said, 'Not really, what advertisement?'

The raven took out a sheaf of printed sheets of paper and handed me one, which said:

All Hail the Visionary Corvus Corax

RAVENOUS PITCHBLACK, ESQUIRE

No. 41, Tree Market, Crow Enclave

We perform calculations of all kinds, audited and edited, retail and wholesale, applying scientific processes. Charge: One inch Re 1. Children half price. Send vital details like your shoe size, if you have earache, and whether you are dead or alive, to receive our catalogue in the mail.

WARNING! WARNING!! WARNING!!!

We lay claim to the pedigreed pure blood of Rex Ravenus—ravens, in other words. All manners of jungle crows, house crows, crowbars, edgar allan crows, etcetera have chosen to run their own business enterprises, lured by lucre. Be warned! Do not allow the allure of their advertising to mislead you.

'So what do you think?' the raven said.

'I couldn't understand all of it,' I replied.

'Yes, it's pretty difficult,' the raven said, 'not everyone gets it. Once there was this client, as bald as a...'

At this the bald old man leapt to his feet in anger. 'You! The next time you talk about bald I'll destroy that slate of yours with my hubble bubble.'

The raven paused, looking flustered, and thought for a bit before saying, 'Not bald, bold, a very bold man, full of courage.'

But even this didn't mollify the old man, who continued grumbling. So the raven said, 'Want to check the accounts?'

Softening, the old man said, 'Done? Yes, let's see it.'

The raven said, 'See it then,' and banged the slate down on the old man's bald head. At once the old man staggered to the ground, clutching his head and pouting, and began to weep, 'Help me, Mum, help me, Auntie, help me, Uncle Shibu,' as he writhed in agony.

Staring at him in surprise, the raven inquired, 'Oh, are you in pain? Was it something you ate?'

At once the old man stopped sobbing and said, 'Nine ten eleven.'

The raven said, 'Twelve.'

Afraid that they were going to start bidding all over again, I quickly said, 'What about the accounts?'

The old man said, 'Yes, that's right, go on, read it out.'

'Quad erat demonstradum crowfidavit scribeth Ravenous Pitchblack, Esquire work orderus. Building shielding document sockument. Descendants shareholders owners possession rights present treasurer manager bookkeeper diarrhoea constipation establishment instruments of settlement. In truth or in falsehood in the lower court or in session court defendant plaintiff witness testimony litigation etcetera or arbitration mediation decree auction notice and all processes...'

Before I could finish, the old man exclaimed, 'What is this nonsense you've written?'

The raven said, 'You have to write these things, or else the accounts won't stand scrutiny. If you want to do your work like a pro you have to have a preamble like this.'

The old man said, 'Good for you, but what's the outcome? You didn't tell me the most important thing.'

The raven said, 'Oh that's been mentioned. You, read the bit at the end.'

What I found near the end was this, written in large letters: seven twos are 14, age 26 inches, deposit 2 kilos and a half, expenditure 37 years.

The raven said, 'It's obviously not an LCM or a GCM. So this is either to be solved by the rule of three or using fractions. On examination two kilos and a half turns out to be a fraction. So the other three add up to the rule of three. Now what I need to know is, do you want fractions or rule of three?'

The old man said, 'Okay then, wait, let me ask.' Bending over, he leaned his head against the tree trunk and began to call softly, 'Booto, can you hear me, Booto?'

After a while someone seemed to answer angrily from inside the tree, 'What do you want?'

The old man said, 'Do you know what Ravenous is saying?'

The answer was still angry. 'What's he saying?'

The old man said, 'He's saying, rule of three or fraction?'

The reply was furious. 'Who's he calling a fraction, you or me?'

The old man said, 'Neither, he's saying, do you want the accounts in rule of three form or in fractions?'

The answer came a little later. 'All right, tell him to make it rule of three.'

Combing his beard with his fingers gravely for a few minutes, the old man said, 'That Booto has no brains. Why should I ask for rule of three? What's wrong with fractions? No, Ravenous, make it fractions.'

The raven said, 'So then if you leave

out the whole two kilos out of two and a half, that leaves a fraction of half kilo, that's your share. Now for the price—if it's unadulterated it's two rupees and eighty-two paise, and if it's diluted with water it's sixteen paise.'

The old man said, 'Three drops of water fell in when I was crying. Here's your slate back, and here's your sixteen paise.'

The raven was thrilled to bits with the money. He began to declaim, 'To baldly go where no crow has ever gone before...'

The old man flew at him in a rage. 'Bald? Again? Just you wait. Booto, can you hear me, Booto? Come quick. He's saying bald again.'

No sooner had he said this than an enormous sack rolled out of the hollow and fell headlong to the ground. I found an old man thrashing about, pinned down by a gigantic shoe. He was identical in appearance to the old man with the hubble bubble.

But instead of helping him up, the first old man climbed up on the shoe and began to pummel the other one furiously with his hubble bubble, saying, 'Get up, get up right now.' Winking at me, the raven said, 'Don't you get it? The boot's on the other foot. And he doesn't want to let go. They fight over this every single day.'

Meanwhile Booto had managed to get to his feet. Brandishing the shoe, he shouted, 'How dare you, you stupid Uto!' At once Uto rolled up his sleeve and shouted back, 'How dare you, you idiotic Booto!'

The raven said, 'Three-two-one box!'

And rightaway thud-thud uff-ouch punch-kick oww-oww. In moments Uto was on his back on the ground, gasping for breath, and Booto was jumping up and down in pain, rubbing his bald head. Now he began to wail, 'Oh my, Uto, oh my brother where have you gone?' Uto joined him promptly, 'Alas and alack, what has happened to our dearest Booto!' Then both of them got up, threw their arms around each other, wept heartily for some time, hugged, and, now in a perfectly good mood, disappeared together inside the hollow in the tree. At this the raven closed his shop and vanished somewhere too.

This was a good time to find my way back home, I was thinking, when I suddenly heard some sort of noise in a bush nearby. Someone was laughing hysterically, simply unable to stop themselves. Peeping in, I discovered a creature—it wasn't clear whether it was a human or a monkey, an owl or a ghost—thrashing about and laughing uncontrollably, saying, 'They'll burst any moment, I'm going to burst my sides laughing any moment now.'

Spotting me, he gathered his breath and got up. 'Thank goodness you turned up, or I'd have exploded with laughter.'

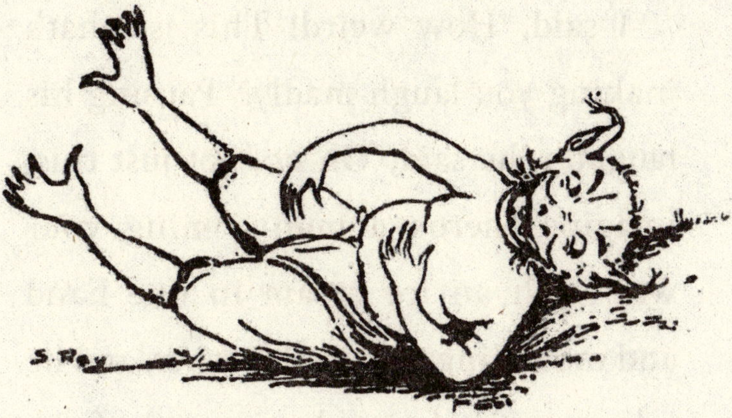

I asked, 'Why're you laughing like you're demented?'

The creature said, 'You want to know why? Imagine the world is flat, and all the water has flowed onto the land, which means the earth has turned to slushy mud everywhere, and everyone is slipping and falling on their faces hahahahaha...' He began to roll on the ground again with laughter.

I said, 'How weird! This is what's making you laugh madly?' Pausing his laughter, he said, 'Oh no, not just this, imagine there's a man coming your way with an ice cream in one hand and modelling clay in the other, and he takes a bite of the clay instead of the ice cream hahahaha...' Another round of laughter.

I said, 'So you're laughing at the possibility of these impossible things and driving yourself crazy?'

He said, 'Not at all, not all of them are impossible. Imagine a man who has pet lizards, feeds and bathes them every day and puts them out to dry, but one day a billy goat appears and eats them all up hahahaha...'

I found the creature's behaviour most peculiar. So I asked, 'Who are you? What's your name?'

After a little thought he replied, 'My name is Hzzbuzzbuzz, my brother's name is Hzzbuzzbuzz, my father's name is Hzzbuzzbuzz, my father's sister's husband's name is Hzzbuzzbuzz…'

'Why not just say every single person in your family is named Hzzbuzzbuzz?'

After some more thought he said, 'That's not true. My name is Tokai. My mother's brother's name is Tokai, my father's brother's name is Tokai, my mother's sister's husband's name is Tokai, my father-in-law's name is Tokai…'

I scolded him, 'Are you telling the truth or are you lying?'

Taken aback, the creature said, 'Er no, my father-in-law's name is Bishkoot.' I got very angry and said spiritedly, 'I don't believe a word of it.'

And before you knew it, without any warning whatsoever, a gigantic goat with a beard peered out from behind the bush, asking, 'Did I hear my name being mentioned?'

I was about to say 'no', but he kept speaking without a break, 'You can say what you like, but there are in fact many things that goats do not eat. Which is why I intend to deliver a speech, whose subject is: Is there anything goats do not eat?' He stepped forward and began his lecture:

'My dear boys and my dearest Hzzbuzzbuzz, as you can tell from the certificate hanging around my neck, my name is Wren And Baartin Singh B.A., food-specialist. I can say baa in the most musical way, which explains why both baa and sing are part of my name. When writing my name in English, I add the B.A., standing for baa. I have examined for myself what is edible and what is not—that is why I have the title of food-specialist. This thing that they say, "madmen bleat and goats eat anything", it is deeply unfair. Why, just a minute ago this wretched fellow was saying billy goats eat lizards. This is an utter lie. I've

tasted many varieties of lizards, there's nothing delicious about them. I admit we do relish many things that you humans don't, like paper bags, or coconut husks, or newspapers, or excellent children's magazines. But we never eat hardback books. It is true we occasionally nibble at blankets and quilts or mattresses and pillows, but those who say we eat beds and tables are lying through their teeth. Sometimes when we're feeling very excited, we munch experimentally on certain things—like pencils and erasers or bottle-caps or dry shoes or canvas bags. I'm told my grandfather once ate half of an Englishman's tent out of sheer euphoria. But that doesn't mean we're partial to knives and scissors or bottles and caps. Some of us enjoy soap, but only unknown soap of poor quality. My younger brother once ate an entire bar of soap...'

Wren And Baartin Singh rolled his eyes upwards at the sky and began to sob piteously. I realized his brother had died an untimely death after consuming the bar of soap.

Hzzbuzzbuzz had been dozing all this time, but he woke up suddenly on hearing the goat's monstrous wailing, shot to his feet and almost choked himself. I honestly thought the fool was going to kick the bucket. But just a few moments later he was thrashing about again, laughing his guts out.

'What's so funny now?' I asked.

He said, 'There was this man, he used to snore so loudly sometimes that everyone was perpetually annoyed with him. One day his house was struck by lightning, and everyone began to beat him up hahahahaha...'

I said, 'Is there no end to your garbage?' and had just turned around when I found someone dressed like a singer, in a tunic and tight pyjamas, his head shaven, smirking at me. The very sight of him irritated me no end. When he realized I had seen him, he cocked his head with a smarmy expression and said, waving his arms, 'Oh no my friend oh no, do not ask me to sing now. I swear on all that I hold dear, my voice will not cooperate with me today.'

I said, 'Don't be a pest! Who asked you to sing?'

But he was so shameless he continued whining next to my ears. 'Are you upset? Oh my dear friend are you upset? All right then, I shall sing a few songs for you, there is no need to be upset my dearest friend, none at all.'

Before I could protest both the goat and that Hzzbuzzbuzz shouted, 'Yessss, let's have some songs.'

At once Shaven Head pulled out two fat sheaves of paper from his pocket, held them close to his eyes and hummed for a few moments before belting out a line in a loud and high voice, 'Red song blue tunes a smiling kind of smell.'

He sang that one line once, twice, five times, ten times. I said, 'This is grating on my nerves, doesn't your song have any other lines?'

Shaven Head replied, 'It does, but that's a different song. That one goes "Dancing down the lane, pavement food is plain, whitewashed with rain." I do not sing it these days. There's another one, "Tender nuts from Nainital," you have to sing it very mildly, I cannot sing this one either at present. The one that I do sing is the "Shifty Sharks" song.

'Misty marks and shifty sharks
all whisper to the sky
Silly bottles, hilly caps, voices running high
Easygoing slanted light on lisping afternoons
Thin and thick and black and white crooning
shadow tunes.'

I said, 'What kind of song is that? From start to finish it makes no sense.' Hzzbuzzbuzz added, 'That's right, it's a very difficult song.' The goat said, 'Not particularly difficult, I just found that bit about silly bottles a little hard to understand, but the rest is easy peasy.'

Shaven Head began to sulk. 'If simple songs are what you were after, you only had to inform me. Do you suppose I am incapable of singing simple ditties?' He began:

The bat said to his friend the hedgehog

Tonight I will show you a ledgedog

I interrupted him, 'There's no such word as ledgedog.'

Shaven Head said, 'Whyever not, there certainly is. If you can have hedgehog or sledge frog or dredge bog then why not ledgedog?'

The goat said, 'Let the song go on meanwhile, we can see about the word later.' At once Shaven Head resumed his singing:

'The bat said to his friend the hedgehog
Tonight I will show you a ledgedog
You will see the owls and insects fly
Around us, the poor mouse will die.
Frogs and tadpoles will just sweat in fright
With teeth that chatter in fear
through the night
Skunks will run with tails between their legs
And you will see the chimbi chango kegs'

I was about to object again, but I stopped myself. The song continued:

'The hedgehog said, did you see or not
The missus sleeping underneath the pot?
A warning for the owl and owless: shut up
If their hooting wakes the missus up
I will poke them till they're full of holes
This is something that they must be told

The bat said if you ask the owls' family
None of them will accept your shamily
Who sleeps in this darkness tinged
with soot?
Your wife is just a fatso and a coot.
And you are getting crazier by the day
A chimney-checking ugly face of clay.'

I don't know if he would have continued singing, but a commotion began at this point. Looking around, I found a crowd had gathered. A hedgehog was whining and sobbing bitterly, and a crocodile in a barrister's wig was thumping him gently on his back with an enormous book of some kind and whispering, 'Don't cry, don't cry, I'll make everything better.' Suddenly a bullfrog with medallions and dressed in a turban brandished a stick and shouted, 'Defamation suit!'

At this a barn owl in a long black gown appeared from nowhere, perched on a large rock and began to nod with his eyes closed, while a gigantic skunk fanned him with a filthy rag. The owl looked around with dim eyes and closed them again at once, saying, 'State the complaint.'

The crocodile screwed up his face with great effort to look like he was going to cry, and rubbed his eyes with his claws till five or six tears oozed out. Then he said in a hoarse voice, 'Your honour, my lord. This is a defamation suit. So first we must understand what a suit is. A suit is a garment, and there can be many kinds—formal suit, bathing suit, safari suit, birthday suit, suit yourself, etcetera.

Because a suit must be well-fitting, we have to see if the complaint fits the...'

Before he could proceed further the jackal in the wig sprang to his feet and said, 'Your honour, a suit is a useless thing. It wears you down to wear it, have you ever seen a hedgehog or a pig in a suit?'

The hedgehog was about to start whining and sobbing again but the crocodile brought the enormous book down on his head with a thud and demanded, 'Got any documents and witnesses?'

The hedgehog nodded towards Shaven Head. 'He has all the documents.'

At this the crocodile snatched Shaven Head's sheaves of songs from his hand and started reading at random:

'One plus one is two
I think I've lost a shoe
A ghost is saying boo
Let's go to the zoo
Make some catfish stew
The sky looks very blue
Got some gum to chew
Fill the cup with glue
Have you got the flu?'

The hedgehog said, 'Oho, not that one, not that one.'

The crocodile said, 'Is that so? All right then, wait.' Pulling out another piece of paper, he began to read:

'Moonlight doomnight banshee aunty
in the shaggy tree
Crunching munching battered heads with

tangy plumthick chutney
Drumstick tree and lipsticked face, the ghouless lurks in stealth
Nose-ring shakes and toenail breaks, what about her health?
Upside down the crone is dangling, hair smelling fresh
Says she, swinging, all those husbands, I will eat their flesh.'

The hedgehog said, 'Oh for heaven's sake. What is this utter bilge you're reading?'

The crocodile cried, 'How about this one then? "Curd with rice, and sour spice, some hair with lice, taste oh so nice..." Oh, not this one either? Wait a minute ... this? "When things are quiet late at night, and I am trying to sleep tight, why these pangs of hunger all the time?" Neither of these, I see. A poem about your wife? You should have told me earlier...

'Have you seen Rambo's wife,
A lioness in real life,
Does the dishes clang trang,
Washes clothes bang bang.

'Fine, this one isn't working either. Then it's got to be this:

'Hacking cough blacking lungs
broken bones kidney stones
Raging fever ageing heart
time to die now say goodbye.'

The hedgehog began to wail helplessly, 'All my money's gone down the drain, what will I do, what an imbecile this lawyer is, can't even find the documents I gave him.'

Shaven Head had been sitting stiffly all this while, suddenly he said, 'Which one do you want, is it this one: "The bat says my dear hedgehog"?'

Perking up, the hedgehog replied, 'Yes! That one!' At once the jackal snarled again, 'What is it the bat says? My lord, let the great bat be summoned as a witness.'

The bullfrog puffed up his cheeks to announce, 'Is the great bat present?' Everyone looked around, but the bat was nowhere to be seen. Then the jackal said, 'In that case, if it please your honour, pass orders for all of them to be hanged.'

The alligator said, 'But why? We're going to appeal.'

The owl said with his eyes closed, 'Let the appeal proceed. Summon the witnesses.'

Looking around, the crocodile asked Hzzbuzzbuzz, 'Want to be a witness? You'll get twenty-five paise.' Leaping to his feet at the prospect of money, Hzzbuzzbuzz took the witness stand and immediately began to chortle.

'Why do you laugh?' asked the jackal.

Hzzbuzzbuzz said, 'There was this witness, he'd been taught to say, you must testify that the book was bound in green, with blue skin near the ears and a red ink-stain on the head. When the cross-examiner asked him, do you know the defendant, he said, I do, he's bound in green, with blue skin near the ears and a red ink-stain on the head hahahahahaha…'

The jackal asked, 'Do you know the hedgehog?'

Hzzbuzzbuzz nodded, 'Oh yes, I know the hedgehog, I know the alligator, I know everyone. Hedgehogs live in burrows, they have long quills, and crocodiles have round scales like mounds, they catch goats and eat them.'

At this Wren And Baartin Singh suddenly burst into tears.

'Now what?' I said.

'A crocodile ate half of my uncle,' he said, 'so the other half died.'

I said, 'Good riddance. Now shut up.'

The jackal said, 'Do you know anything about litigation?'

Hzzbuzzbuzz answered, 'Of course I do. Someone makes an accusation, he's the plaintiff, he has a lawyer, then they bring an ant from somewhere. He's the defendant, he has a lawyer too. There are ten witnesses on each side. And there's a judge, who sits there and sleeps.'

The owl said, 'Of course I'm not sleeping—I have an eye disease so I keep them closed.'

Hzzbuzzbuzz retorted, 'I've seen plenty of judges, all of them have an eye disease,' and began to laugh in a most offensive way.

'What is it now?'

Hzzbuzzbuzz said, 'There was a man who wasn't right in his head, he used to give names to everything. His shoes were called antidisestablishmentarianism, his umbrella was named floccinaucinihilipilification, his bathroom was called pseudopseudohypoparathyroidism—but as soon as he named his house pneumonoultramicroscopicsilicovolcanoconiosis there was an earthquake and everything collapsed at once hahahahaha...'

The jackal said, 'Is that so? What's your name?'

'Right now my name is Hzzbuzzbuzz.'

'What do you mean right now, does a name change with time?'

Hzzbuzzbuzz said, 'Are you telling me you don't know that? In the morning my name is Alnarkel, and when we get close to evening it will become Remmingtree.'

'Where do you live?'

Hzzbuzzbuzz said, 'Did you mention Olive? She's gone back home.'

At once Uto and Booto shouted in the crowd, 'Then Olive must be dead.' Uto said, 'People die like flies when they go back home.' Booto said, 'As soon as Habul's father's younger brother went home we heard he was dead.' The jackal said, 'Don't all talk together, it's very confusing.' At this Uto told Booto, 'The next time you talk together I'll beat you to a pulp.' Booto said, 'The next time you make trouble I'll bundle you into my boot.'

The jackal declared, 'My lord, all these people are lunatics and dunces, their testimony is worthless.' The crocodile began to thrash the ground with his tail in anger at this, saying, 'Who says they're worthless? They're being paid a full twenty-five paise to appear as witnesses.' Counting out the money, he immediately handed it to Hzzbuzzbuzz. Overhead, someone said, 'Witness No. 1, cash price twenty-five paise.' I looked up to find Ravenous writing down the accounts.

The jackal continued, 'Do you know anything else on the subject?'

Hzzbuzzbuzz pondered over things for a bit and then said, 'There's a song about jackals that I know.'

'And what song might that be?'

Hzzbuzzbuzz began to chant, 'Come one come all, brinjal for the jackal, no salt and pepper at all...'

At this the jackal sprang to his feet and said, 'Never mind, that's a different jackal, your testimony is done.'

Meanwhile what had happened was that the sight of a witness getting paid had led to a rush among bystanders to be witnesses. Just as everyone began to push and shove one another, Ravenous dropped down from the tree, perched in the witness's box and began to give his testimony.

Before anyone could question him he rattled off, 'All Hail The Visionary Corvus Corax, Ravenous Pitchblack, Esquire, No. 41, Tree Market, Crow Enclave, we perform calculations of all kinds, audited and edited, retail and wholesale...'

The jackal said, 'Stop this nonsense at once, just answer my questions. Name?' The raven said, 'What a pain! That's exactly what I was telling you, Ravenous Pitchblack, Esquire.'

'Residence?'

'I told you didn't I, Raven Enclave.'

'How far away is that?'

'Hard to say. In terms of hours, twenty-five paise, in terms of miles, ten paise. Two paise discount if you pay cash. Eighty paise by addition, thirty by subtraction, seven by division, twenty-one rupees by multiplication.'

'Enough with your showing off. My question is: do you know your way home or not?'

'You bet I do, there it is, right in front of us.'

'How far does this road go?'

'How can the road go anywhere? The road stays just where it is, can a road wander about? Does it go to Darjeeling for a change of air?'

'I must say you are most impudent. So you want to be a witness. What do you know about litigation?'

'What a question! Who's been doing the accounts all this time? I can tell you anything and everything you want to know. Let's begin with defamation suits. Formal suits, bathing suits, safari suits, birthday suits. What happens when you wear them? Jackals look ridiculous, but not crows and ravens. Then there was a witness, cash price twenty-five paise, he was witless, the skin of his ears turned blue—that's known as kala-azar. Then there was a man who used to give everything a name, he'd call jackals oilthieves, crocodiles octaawkwards, owls traitorkings...'

At this there was bedlam in the crowd. The crocodile lost his temper and swallowed the bullfrog, which made the skunk screech at the top of his voice. The jackal picked up an umbrella to shoo the raven away. The owl said solemnly, 'Silence everyone, I shall now deliver my verdict.' Turning to a rabbit with a pen tucked in behind its ear, he ordered, 'Write down, defamation suite no. 24. Plaintiff: the hedgehog. Defendant, rise to your feet. Where's the defendant?'

Everyone said, 'Oh no, we clean forgot, there's no defendant.'

Shaven Head was quickly coaxed into becoming the defendant. The idiot assumed the defendant would be paid too, just like witnesses, and didn't object.

The verdict was three months in jail and seven days of hanging for Shaven Head. I was considering protesting against such an unjust judgment when the billy goat bleated 'Wren And Baartin' and butted me. Then he proceeded to bite my ear.

Everything became a blur. The goat's face gradually changed into my uncle's. I realized he was boxing my ear, saying, 'So you've been sleeping while pretending to study your Wren and Martin grammar book?'

I was utterly baffled. At first I thought I'd been dreaming all this while, but I know you won't believe this, when I looked for my handkerchief it was nowhere to be found, and a cat who was perched on the fence licking his whiskers scrambled down to the ground and ran away when he saw me.

And from the garden at the back a goat cried out 'baaaa'.

I told another uncle all of this, but he dismissed me, saying, 'Don't tell me all these silly stories you dreamt up.'

People turn so fatheaded when they grow old they refuse to believe anything. But none of you is all that old yet, so I'm trusting you and telling you what happened.

MORE STORIES AND POEMS

Translated by

SUDESHNA SHOME GHOSH

No Fear, Come Here

Don't be afraid, come come, I will not hurt you,
Listen, in a boxing match, could I ever defeat you?
My heart is so kind, I have never known anger,
I will chomp you up? That will happen never!
These horns on my head have scared you silly—
I may be crazy but I have never butted like a billy.

Come come, into my home, stay for a day or four,
I will pet you night and day as soon as you walk
through the door.
Is the club in my hand the reason for your fright?
This club is so light it will not hurt you one mite!

Stop being a ninny, or should I catch you by your legs?

When I sit on your head, don't you try to beg!

I'm there, wifey is there, so are my sons nine—

All of us will bite you if you don't stop your whines!

Dashu's Mystery Box

Everyone in our school knew Dashu the Crazy. Even those who didn't know anyone else, had heard of him. Once, a new guard started working at the school. He was from some village—an innocent and naïve rustic. But even he could recognise Dashu the Crazy from the get go, although he had only heard of him before.

It was easy to pick Dashu out from a crowd of boys. His appearance, the way he talked, the way he walked, everything indicated that he was a little 'cuckoo' in the head. His eyes were round, his ears unnaturally large, and he had a headful of unruly curly hair. Looking at his appearance, it seemed:

A stick figure with a messy, pumpkin head
Looks like a scarecrow has appeared instead

When he spoke nineteen to the dozen, very fast, or waved his arms about and danced around in excitement, he reminded us of a rather large lobster.

It was not that Dashu was stupid. While doing Maths, especially long sums that needed lots of addition and subtraction, he was extremely clever. And sometimes he would come up with so many elaborate ways to play pranks on us that we would be astonished at his intelligence.

When ‘Dashu’, or to tell his actual name Dasharathi, first joined our school, Jagabandhu was the ‘good boy’ of the class. Though he was very good in his studies, none had seen someone as mean and cowardly as Jagabandhu.

One day, Dashu asked Jagabandhu the meaning of an English word. Without any reason, Jagabandhu started scolding Dashu: ‘Do you think I have no other work? Today I have to teach you English, tomorrow someone will ask me to do their sums, the day after someone else will come with another demand—is this what I will do all day?’

Dashu got very mad and shouted back, 'You are a mean, nasty person.'

Promptly Jagabandhu complained to our class teacher: 'The new boy is saying bad words.'

And the teacher scolded Dashu so much that after that he dared not say anything more.

Our English teacher was Bishtu Babu and Jagabandhu was his favourite student. While teaching, if Sir ever needed to check something in the textbook, he would always ask Jagabandhu to give his book. One day, while teaching, he asked to see the Grammar book. Jagabandhu immediately rushed up to give his book, which was covered with a green-coloured paper. Bishtu Babu opened the book and his face turned thunderous. He asked, 'Whose book is this?'

Jagabandhu proudly proclaimed, 'Mine, Sir.'

'Hmm, so you are studying from a new edition, is it? The whole book has changed!'

Bishtu Babu read out the name of the book he was holding: **Yashwant the Valiant Policeman, A Hair-raising Detective Novel.**

Jagabandhu, who had still not understood what had happened, stared foolishly at the teacher. Bishtu Babu glared at him fiercely and asked, 'From where have you learnt all this nonsense behaviour?'

While Jagabandhu tried to stammer

an explanation, Bishtu Babu shut him up with a single rebuke, 'Enough! There's no need to behave as if you don't know anything!'

Jagbandhu's ears turned red with embarrassment and shame. We were quite pleased to see this. Later, we got to know that the whole thing was our dear Dashu's doing. He had replaced the Grammar book with a similarly sized book with the exact same green cover.

~

We would always tease Dashu by making fun of his looks and his crazy behaviour. But he was never annoyed by this. Sometimes he would himself add to the stories, poking fun at his own deeds.

One day, Dashu said, 'Friends, whenever anyone makes mango candy in our neighbourhood, they call me. Do you know why?'

We asked, 'Is it because you can eat a lot of the mango candy?'

He shook his head. 'No. It's because the candy has to be laid out on the terrace in the sun to dry up first. If I show my face there, the crows in the area get the fright of their lives and fly away cawing in fear. So then my neighbours don't need to guard the candy anymore.'

One time, Dashu came to school wearing very baggy trousers instead of the usual dhoti, which was part of our uniform. They looked like pyjamas, and he had paired them up with a blazer that looked more like a pillow cover. He looked so weird! Dashu knew he was looking really strange, and he thought the whole thing was really funny.

When we asked him, 'Hey Dashu, what's with those pants?'

He replied with a grin, 'So I can learn English better.'

Another time, he shaved his head and tied a bandana on his head and came to school. When we laughed seeing this new look, he joined in with the laughter as well.

Dashu did not have a musical bone in his body. He could not sing to save his life. Everyone knew this, including him. Yet, when the School Inspector came to visit, Dashu decided to serenade him by singing very loudly and off-key. If any of us had done this, we would have been roundly scolded and punished. But no one said anything to Dashu because everyone knew he was The Crazy One.

~

When we returned to school after the vacations, we saw that Dashu had come carrying a large box.

Our teacher asked, 'Dashu, what have you brought in that box?'

Dashu said, 'Sir, all my things.'

Things? What things could these be? We started whispering among ourselves. Dashu already had his books, notebooks, pencils and sharpeners with him. So what did he mean by 'things'?

When we asked him, he did not give us a proper reply. Instead he clutched the box tightly to himself and said, 'Don't you dare! None of you touch my box!' Then he unlocked the box with a key, opened the lid an inch, peered inside and nodded solemnly to himself saying, 'That's good.' After that he started mumbling to himself as if he was calculating something. When I went to peek in, the crazy fellow swiftly turned the box away from me and locked it up again.

Soon, a huge discussion began among all of us.

One person said, 'That must be his tiffin box. He has brought food in it.' But none of us had ever seen Dashu bring food to school or eat anything.

Someone else said, 'That must be his money bag. He keeps all his money in that. That is why he keeps it close to himself.'

But then somebody else said, 'Who needs such a huge box to keep money? Is he planning to start a moneylending business in school?'

The next day, during recess time, Dashu came up to me busily and gave me the key to the box.

He said, 'Keep this carefully. Mind, you don't lose it. And if I am late in returning, give it to the guard before you go to the classroom.' Then he took his box and kept it in the guard's room.

We were so thrilled! Finally we would solve the mystery of Dashu's mystery box. Now all we had to do was wait for the guard to go out of the room.

Soon, the guard picked up his stove on which he made his lunch chapattis and some more vessels and went to the backyard to wash them by the tap. We were waiting for just this to happen. No sooner had the guard rounded the corner than five-seven of us entered his room and pulled out Dashu's box towards us. I took out the key Dashu had given me and opened the box.

Inside, there was a mysterious looking bundle of paper, tied up with a piece of cloth. We undid the knots and found that there was another paper box inside. On opening that we found yet another smaller box. Opening that, we found a card.

On one side of the card were the words: **Fooled you!**

On the other side: **Too much curiosity is bad for your health.**

Dumbfounded, we stared at each other's faces.

Finally, one boy said, 'This fellow has made a nice fool of us.'

Another said, 'Let's tie up the bundle exactly the way it was so that he doesn't know we opened it. That way we will fool him.'

I said, 'Fine, when he comes, make sure to act all innocent and ask him again and again to show us what's inside the box.'

We quickly put back everything exactly the way it was and closed the box. But as I was about to lock it, we heard a sound.

'Ho ho ho ho ho!'

Startled, we turned around and saw Dashu sitting on the adjoining wall and laughing as if he would burst. That sly fox! He had been spying on us this whole time! Now we understood. Giving me the keys, keeping the box with the guard, pretending to leave the school—all these were just part of his act. He had been lugging that box to school just so he could fool us like this!

Now do you understand, why we call him 'Dashu, The Crazy One'?

Don't Laugh, Ramgoru Calf

Those Ramgoru calves have been told not to laugh
Tell them something punny,
They will scream, 'Please, nothing funny!'

The worry always niggles— Hark, someone has giggled
Carefully with one eye
They watch sharp as a spy.

To sleep, they cannot be so bold, all day themselves they scold:
'If you dare even joke
Your eyes I will poke!'

On branches they dare not rest or go to the forest
Oh it would be such a pickle
If the cool breeze gave a tickle.

Baskets of worry fill their minds   in the corners of clouds if they find

Laughter droplets that glisten

With ears pricked up they listen.

Hidden in the bushes dark   fireflies glimmer and spark

In rhythm very fine

To laughter they keep time.

All those who are hopping,   laughing, giggling and chortling

The Ramgoru is very hurt

Understand that first.

Their house is filled up   with scolding loud and sharp,

There's no place there

For whiffs of laughter-filled air.

Crackers in a Pot

It was our friend Ramapada's birthday and he had come to school with a big pot of mihidana sweets. As soon as the bell rang for recess, we crowded around him and took turns dividing the sweets amongst us. The only one who would not take a share was Dashu the Crazy.

It's not like Dashu did not like mihidanas. But he and Ramapada were sworn enemies, and they were often fighting about something or the other.

We all told Ramapada, 'Give a little mihidana to Dashu.'

Ramapada went to Dashu and said, 'Hey Dashu, want to eat? But you better make sure you never fight with me again, okay? I will give you some sweets then.'

Who wouldn't get angry if someone talks to them like this? But Dashu did not say a word. He solemnly took a handful of the sweets, called out to the security guard's pet goat, and fed all his mihidana to it. Then, smiling secretly, he looked inside the pot of sweets for some time, before walking out of the school, thinking who knows what! We finished what was left in the pot and started playing. No one bothered about Dashu or wondered what he was up to.

After the tiffin break, when we returned to class, we found Dashu sitting quietly in a corner, solving sums. I could not help but wonder what he was planning.

I asked him, 'Have you done something?'

Dashu looked at me innocently and said, 'Yes, two GCM sums.'

I said, 'Oh, who wants to know about Maths! Are you planning a prank?'

Dashu got really angry when he heard this. The teacher too had just arrived and Dashu was ready to complain to him about us. Somehow we calmed the crazy fellow down and made him sit back in his seat.

Our teacher was not a bad sort. He

was usually in no hurry to start with the lessons. Only, if we got too noisy, he would suddenly fly into a rage. At that time, his temper would rise rapidly and he would scold us terribly. That day, he sat down and told us to work on our grammar. Then, he promptly settled back comfortably and fell fast asleep. We all opened our books and pretended to read aloud. In reply, we heard his nose make a beautiful 'ghrrr-ghrrr' sound as he snored. We loved this sound, as we then knew he had floated away nicely into sleepland. With opportunity at hand, we forgot all about our grammar books and instead took out our slates and started playing noughts and crosses. Whenever the snoring sound went down, we quickly whipped out our books and in a calming lullaby recited the verbs. That sent him right back to sleep like a baby.

While everyone was busy playing, Dashu was sitting in a corner doing something. None of us paid him the least attention. However, after a while, a 'phutt' sound came from under the platform on which our teacher's chair was placed.

Our teacher sat up, and looking around sleepily, said an annoyed 'Oh!' He looked like he was getting ready to say more, when...Dhadam! Crack! Pop! Fizz! All sorts of loud sounds started coming from under his chair. It was so loud that it felt like the school was shaking, as if all the carpenters in the world had decided to hammer in nails and had started sawing here, right now, at the same time. For a long time, we just stared, stunned into silence, our mouths hanging open.

Our teacher jumped up in the air and with a horrible yelp leaped across the table and landed right in the middle of the classroom. We had seen the inter-school high-jump champ Nabin Pal doing many fantastic jumps. But even he had never attempted such a jump before. In the next room, the younger students were shouting out their five times tables. They too stopped in alarm. Everywhere in the school, people started shouting and jumping and running around in fear. Even the guard's dog took up the refrain and barked at the top of its voice, adding to the chaos.

After five minutes of this awful noise, when the chaos subsided and it became quiet, our teacher asked in

a very angry voice, 'Where did that noise come from?'

The guard came with a long stick, poked under the platform, and pushed out a pot.

It was Ramapada's pot of sweets! Stray bits of mihidana were still stuck around its mouth.

The teacher frowned and asked, 'Whose pot is this?'

Innocent Ramapada spoke up, 'Sir, it is mine.'

And that's it—two hands immediately seized both of Ramapada's ears and gave them a nice twist.

'What did you bring in the pot?' the teacher shouted.

By then, Ramapada had understood

that he was going to get blamed for all that had happened. The poor thing quickly tried to explain, 'But Sir, there was mihidana in that. I don't...'

Before he could finish, Teacher roared, 'And those mihidana turned themselves into crackers and started bursting themselves, didn't they?' Two tight slaps landed on Ramapada's cheeks soon after.

By now the other teachers had also gathered in our classroom. They too looked ready to land a few slaps on him. Poor Ramapada! He was going to get badly punished for no fault of his.

Amidst all this commotion, suddenly Dashu picked up my slate and said, 'Sir, see! While you were sleeping, they were all playing noughts and crosses.'

My name could be seen clearly on the slate, so Teacher raised his hand to give me one huge slap as well. But then, he stopped. He glared at Dashu instead. 'And who said I was sleeping?'

Dashu stared at him, puzzled. Then he answered, 'But, you were snoring…'

Teacher quickly changed the subject. 'And what were you doing? While they were all playing?'

Dashu declared with a cheerful grin, 'Oh, I was lighting the crackers, of course!'

Everyone stared at him. What was the boy saying!

For almost half a minute no one said anything. Then Teacher roared, 'Why were you lighting the crackers?'

Dashu was not one to be scared. He pointed to Ramapada and said, 'Why didn't he want to share his mihidana with me?'

Hearing this weird logic, Ramapada shouted back, 'It's *my* mihidana. I will give it to whoever I please!'

Dashu immediately replied, 'Then, it is *my* cracker! I will also do as I please.'

Who can argue with a crazy boy? All the teachers gave us a few final rounds of scolding and then left for their classrooms. Because Dashu is 'The Crazy One', he was not punished.

After school, we all tried to explain to Dashu why what he had done was wrong. But he just did not agree. He said, 'My crackers, Ramapada's pot of sweets. If I am to blame, then so is Ramapada. He deserved to have his ears boxed. Bas!'